W9-CCD-633

TEREBINTHOS
Poems and Stone Fragments

Gordon Walmsley

Salmon Poetry

Published in 1999 by
Salmon Publishing Ltd,
Cliffs of Moher, Co. Clare, Ireland
http://www.salmonpoetry.com
email: salpub@iol.ie

© Gordon Walmsley 1999
The moral right of the author has been asserted.

A catalogue record for this book is available from the British Library.

The Arts Council
An Chomhairle Ealaíon

Salmon Publishing gratefully acknowledges the financial assistance of The Arts
Council of Ireland and Helge Fonden/The Helge Foundation, Denmark.

ISBN 1 897648 46 4 Softcover

Cover photography & design by Brenda Dermody
Set by Siobhán Hutson
Printed by Techman Ireland Ltd., Dublin

To V.J.W.

Acknowledgements

"Sensing Sophia" first appeared on the website Morgan's Supreme Beings, excerpted from the then unpublished book, Terebinthos.

Contents

LIFTINGS

III

For if they do these things in a green tree,
what shall be done in the dry?

– King James version (Luke)

To speak really right
is to peel a gauze
from what we see
to hear
a pulse behind
it is much more like music
deeply woven
hidden among the three blue stones
between your voice
and the blood's most natural cradle
three tones
telling the sun to move its head
so as not to block the light

I

Listening to everything around us
we can wonder
what the wind would never tell

a child in Baghdad is a child
in Berlin is a child
in dark Brussels

where the wind never tells

A stork
  folds its wings
    blending grasses with summer

as shadows
  pass over
    words falling into us

unable to discern
  we take the tinctured thoughts
    as our own

  willing to fight for them
we bury them in the black fields

Winds, with the great trees wild
with big breaths

Whose feet will stand
near toppled wheat
or run down paths
to woods
darkened with rain?

The swells of the sea seem very near
you can hear them through the trees
yet the sands beneath
crystalline waters
are a long way off

                    and close to remembering,
sounds of the wood owl echoing still,
blossoming in the fields of silence

and passing the beach of the thirteen crescents
swans, grey with youth, or white
with something I do not know –
drifting towards the April sounds of the guns

THE TIME OF THE SWANS

In the time of the swans

men came running

with broken tongues

they told us stories

we tried to understand them

before the ashes would fall through the mountains

or sounds of the oaks would engulf us

or bandits would bully the terrified messengers

in the time of the swans

we covered our eyes

so our ears would not hear

but we left our mouths untouched

and high above the dark time's sobbings

we called to the swans

and they answered us

high above the dark time's sobbings

but we could not hear them

because we had bound our eyes

Enchantress

Near rocks
where feet run in summer
between a sea as great as possibility
and a lake
rooming two hearts
I met an enchantress, a mover of winds, proud
because she could see giants casting stones
into the flowing waters leaves
where I could only wade
carrying a lamp before me
with water rising past my ankles

Flinging her arms before me
she warned
how illusions could charm me
since no song can be perfect
as long as jewels
fall through waters
disturbing
mirrors

And what were my careful probings, ha!
my eyes following lappings
as a child follows watery seams along the sands
what were they
to visions.
I should listen to her.
and all would be well.

Then she who is with me
placed her hand on my arm
and she said to the enchantress:

Though we seldom see what falls from the hands
of gods and demons
our eyes can follow lappings on the sands
and as a child we can try to tell
what makes the waves unravel as they do
hastily sometimes
in a bunch
or tranquilly
as though it were a southern breeze
and little more
than silence moving her hand over the water
bringing ripples

She who is with me says ...

I will tell you something strange.
of a small pond
with a carriage of gold
sinking through
bottom mud

we walk along a path
leading out to where the view grows larger
between the pond
and the great waters washing the lime cliffs

there where the view is fine
we break up the earth
so the sun can be there
we drop in seeds
pale as shadowed
skin

before a wall
we meet our sisters
gravely, without speaking ...
somehow we know we will meet
many times
we will plant and dig
and bring the green things home
yet we know too
this time will always be the golden moment
though the pond scarcely seen
will be what we most remember

Meetings

Where the flower
meets the cross
or the kneeling chronicler
tells us of how things
have come to be
or what was two
becomes three
not because something new is born
but because blue meets green
in lemon gold
or because
the owl did not see
or the swan glided through
what our eyes made
or we noticed
the lovely gait of the gods
in the belled ankles
of the mother of flowers
fleeing the razored mountains
from the children of terror

II

What Is Loosed

Hero sees her in the mirroring shield.
Or he enters the maze with a thread in his hand.
The box once opened is hard to close.
And the moths are whirling, whirling.

Swarms come upon us now and then.
I think they are from Asia.
Exotic species not now known.
In the new times, whirling, whirling.

And even our friends, even our friends,
Our friends are no longer careful.
They bring down clouds to darken our heads.
Having grown blind.
Being born blind.

And swirling their legs the storm lets loose upon us
With vexious currents voluming the red-wind
They would sweep us higher than the rainy heavens
Were it not for our love of this crazy earth
And the gift of a mirror
To keep us straight.

Sometimes
Saying no word
We let our friends drive crimson horses
Over the most amazing seas
With the moth wings fluttering the wave tops
In the new times whirling, whirling

in the time it takes a shadow

to disappear into light

worlds can go under

Statement

It was a very reasonable war.
We had an enemy. We deemed him evil.
When the world's spotlight was on him
We could see him killing.
His men took over a country
We bought oil from.
It was reasonable we could not allow this.
We threatened our machine would kill.
He had his chance.
We turned on our machine.
It was a very good machine.
It killed over three hundred and thirty-six thousand.
But the best was we could hide behind it.
We could kill without ourselves getting killed.
This was only reasonable.
We had to protect our own.
A European said we are a country
Quick to anger, slow to compassion.
I hope that is not true.
But truth is something I do not want to consider.
And besides,
It is too much bound up
With two words I hate:
Conscience
and
I.
And that is only reasonable.

Thresholding

When even the smallest subterfuge is illumined

Balloons before all eyes

When just about everyone

Knows what everyone else is up to

Can see through the sad fumblings of politicians

Giving their best "cheese"

Before the blue backdrop of lastingness –

It is there we see Darkman

Drawing into himself

The shadows of our hands

Looming

Before the cradle of veils

So we are riveted

By our blossomings

to treat the silence

with greatest care

drawing out the golden threads

hanging them before the sun

... making ... chimes ...

INKLINGS OF DARKMAN

Some God

If a god were to hold

revenge up before us

as a blade and the words

    esteem getting even

or if he would bellow how large he was

and that we should be terrified and

only obey

then we might better see him

as he-shining-dimly

in nights cold as numbering can be

or heat

blind as day

Pure Intelligence

With the whole world breaking open
Who will be the master of shards?
and will glass splinters
Reassemble, as tiny chips of intelligence?
Who will reign
                    from heights
                                Absolutely Intelligent
Unencumbered
                by something
                            so clumsy
                                    as a breathing heart?
The Master of Shards is certain
chips themselves
will sport
little chip crowns
and a million shimmering heads
will proclaim an Intelligence
more smoothly calculated
than our own could ever be
burdened as we are
with holding the middle
between the hand that falls or rises
                                and words both light
and dark

Gusts

She came running –
cold day in Denmark
thin cotton skirt
full of pale flowers
dragging black sack
black sack before her
all I could see, see it was bursting
plastic toys
toys on a cold day

Voice she used, unused
to speaking, came in dry bursts, bursts
blowing busstops
    Bus does it come, come to the
    sick house?
Strange she was strange, too strange to find
Answer. And your name is what, said a
poet near silence, thin cotton shirt,
falling to whiteness.
    Denmark. She said. Cold day in Denmark.
    Bursting my flowers. Bus to the sick house.

we arrived in the fog

and when we left

smoke had veiled

every single tree

Cobalt Blue

When wisdom's shadows
   fled into the ice-forms
      giants swayed
         foot to foot, bringing fire
           to burning
              cities

For once again
   The Peace-Maker was at work.
      Gathering robes about him
         He began by proclaiming freedom
           In the dark language of flames.
When wisdom's shadows
fled into the ice-forms

That the word compassion
Might never more be spoken
He stretched his arm till it grew stiff
Leadening his fingers
round
a torch's
throat
When wisdom's shadows
fled into the ice-forms

31

Then he set a crown upon his head.
Not a crown of thorns.
But similar.
And he had electric light
blaze between the spikes
    EXULTING
High above the frozen millions
When wisdom's shadows
fled into the ice-forms

When wisdom's shadows
fled into the ice-forms
all the children were
fast asleep
and some of the grownups
too
giants were bringing fire
to burning cities
It was all they could do!
When wisdom shadows
fled into the ice-forms

Closings

Basilica.
with the walls torn off –
where a Host once brightened
obsidian slabs
vaults now rise
over open-air ruins

and the children, the children ... milling about

This was once G.
Betrayer of words
Laws
Hardened down.
Down into stone.
Slabs hung frozen.
Near heat of two temples.
Welded they make.
A scooped-out.
Cranium.

Open-air.

A church that is skeletoned.
Bones giving lustre
To July's white heat.
Bones
ably
scattered.

Try to remember
Basilica's old self.
Was he a giant
lumbering among orange groves,
ravening peels from the high fruits
... scattering them?

Children come.
They are looking for something.
In grown-up socks, tall as you and I.
But what they are looking for
cannot be found
among these broken
stones.
And the servers of bread
are a hopeless lot
stumbling among the wedding guests
insisting on the original ovens
despite the recent
taint.

Basilica
with the walls torn off
where a Host once brightened
lengthening slabs
vaults rise scooped
over open-air ruins
and the children, the children ... milling about ...

Murk Mass Six

The exhilaration of tittering cables.

Think of all you can get!

Televisions   Telephones

Melting together   World-Wide   Chips

Information

Blitzing before you

                                        Everything

You want   *All the things*

You can get!

And think of all the ways you can imagine!

Pictures

Stimulating   pictures

ALLLLLL WILL BE GIVEN YOU!

I do not want your soul. No. You.

Have that. I do not want your.

Immortal soul.

I just. I just.

Do not want you to notice.

Him.

LIFTINGS

rocks still gleam through silken glass

and the pond still moves

displacing the notched centuries

Breakings

Roots and rocks
pathing a pond
where the black loon dives

if she returns
it will be to break open worlds
these mountains enclose

waiting till the sun swells, filling,
we cross a bridge
into the moss fields

there we find only sand
and night
sweeping the forest blue

through the tiniest of windows
trees block a lighthouse
sea eagles know

light from the island
no longer moves
tree tops
or walls of this room

nor do doors close as tight
as once they did close
when you swept over the trees at night
calling the diving loon

Carding Light

I imagine you with a net of gleaming threads
sometimes you let it sweep along the sea-floss
sometimes you spread it out beneath the night
or you move it back and forth
as an enchantress
steals sun glints
showering
our eyes
or you draw through the deep sea swells
pulling forth a tapestry full of sparklings
I see in their forms
gestures difficult to catch –
to get hold of them
I would have to break the shine
you let englobe me

If you have something to do with the sea
it is this:

phosphorous streaks by the bow
when the world is a feathered darkness –
you let the light out
in strange evanescences, in strange patterns,
furtive sometimes and a magic
difficult to break through

If you have something to do with heavens
it lies in the mysteries of the jingling wave froth
the bubbles gliding down watery valleys
then off again –
and the earth
what do you have to do with the earth
with those of us who walk upon it
sway above it at night
sink under it, learning?
Were I to answer
I would have to find a good rock
to stand upon
so the waves could recognize themselves
as water
a stone I could stand on
so I could think
with a warm light
different from your own
because the shapes
you let move in me
are difficult to catch
tough to get hold of –

If I call you Neptune
it is because you are the night's night
glittering the sea with swift fishes
in blind spots of the eyeless
a world of words
and soundings, bell-buoys
echoing through tides by the green sea mists

Sacrament

A sign? A pointing finger? A quotation?
A book cleaves open to just the right place:
John. Near the well, the old well of Jacob.
And our dear most present lord.
He is resting by the well at the sixth hour.
She comes too, lightly, without sandles,
Says in the older English
The English of darkened brass:
   How is it that thou, being a Jew
   asketh drink of me
   which am a woman of Samaria?

It is a passage a friend often shows me.
To point the way in the time of flags,
Uniforms, insignias, and the bent ones
Emptying their hearts into the streets.
Deeper. Let us go deeper.
Too late for nonsense.
What is *division* she might now ask,
sending her question along the silver
thread, its strands spiralling upwards, visible,
invisible, then visible again, becoming
lavender and orange and red
at times visible, unseen, then seen
again, disappearing towards the cresting night
into an angel's bright hair, the wandering thread that is
spiralling always
spiralling

She waits
and she knows to wait.
Attentive to the stirrings.
Knows the sacredness of questioning:
That a question, when elevated,
Becomes a sacrament.

43

I asked
who are you dear one
and why do you come
with sadness all around you
and one bent knee?
Is the bearer of crowns
too much himself
and no fit vessel
for what gods can bring?
and are there no hearts
you can curl up in
to fill with bright dreams?

III

Listening

Some say your fields are windless
so if you visit
you may not feel the airs around you
yet they are the breath of our being, these winds …

The moon in the north can be starless
and as we walk along the road going all the way
to the little tower …
high above the stables
doves
above the shifting horses …
a swan unfolds its wings above a white wall
lengthening above the flowers of spring,
rubies, amber, and jasmine too …
in this night
there is a long wall
whitening …
as the moon's most delicate fingers
let fall a blue most silken veil
it descends to embrace the sunken land
where the fields are often starless

It may be true

your place is a place of no wind

where no waves trail thin threads along the sand grains

(they hold the secrets of our age)

nor the clatter of gulls, jeering, jeering

But where you are there is a silence

like the shattered earth we will one day console

silence

covering fields

that never move

violet

and

very

still

She looked at me
with eyes calm as tempered blood:
It is not that they could not know
. real wisdom
if given
but they don't even look for it
or value it … [precious] …
only real wisdom
can keep them
– not from destruction –
surely some will survive
most alluring madness …
but from becoming
wholly
bestial

What Is Born

Not seeing very far
they couldn't say the right words

deaf to the round tones of bells
they could hear neither warnings

nor peals of celebration
(as when love is born between tides)

on flat screens of glass, the cold's
alluring mists and sharp noisings

parodies of the human voice
pressed into tubes

had formed sounds come
they would have been too big for shrivelled souls

small ones were better
easier to swallow or slough off

and they could be twisted into shapes
layed out in books

rolled into lines
and called poetry

though there would be nothing of poetry in them
nothing of the sea

near to men's hearts
nor of footsteps

sounding down earth ways
echoing into the sun

in making words they would forget the Word
and so be consigned to the lesser mysteries

but that was not necessarily a bad thing
learning would go on, tumbling here (nations, cites)

standing up over there (unexpected groupings)
fools would die

to be born, hungering for wisdom, on the ocean's seam
to learn one day that each man harbours a babbler

he spends a lifetime
trying to reform

and words are his rightful means

do you fear
when the horn sounds noon
bearing Christ through the low streets
like a shadow bearing midnight
half alone

Symposion

A moon washing the night sky white.
Yet because the moon is near the trees, and down
to a quarter, stars are as clear as a finished thought
clear as a pentagram, as a square, or triangle
and more than lines, or a level plane

Clarity. The night moon flooding a curving.
Something so secret as not to be spoken.

A sculptor of words
reckoned conversation as highest –
greater than love, greater even than light.
It is hard to imagine
conversation could be greater
than the light that touches me
though speaking with you
can open
a night

Solutions
no one man can find them.
We live in a time of
many rules.
Parliaments sit perplexed
dreaming up laws.
What was Caesar's
runs through Caesar's
fingers

finds its way into sucking caverns
splitting slopes of the red volcanoes

While the spirit of Me. Me.
Magnetic Me.
is taking, taking.
We have a task
no less
than turning rivers around
that we may emerge from under the weight of lines
electrical
heavily fallen

A web is often hard to lift.

Yet we stand
the night clearly round us
men and women
on earth

We can speak to each other.

Sensing Sophia

Is it true
the great hierarchy of giving beings
is different now
the ladder tipped and rounded
to become a bridge
and that we walk together with angels
to and fro, easily companionable
and seraphims
breathing to either side of us
taking our hands in their hands
so we can close them
so we can let them open
no longer cupping them
above our eyes
but lowering them
to where the heart is still?

That we stand now on the same broad ground as
cherubims, dominions and other shaping beings
to create from this earth
something to lift up
something our hands can raise
or set down
among amethyst spirals
because we would have it that way
is that true?
or that angels breathe almost as we breathe
make mistakes as we would falter
know tears
as we would be sad
know resolve
as we would lend them our hands
to break the leadening dome
we sense may soon enclose us
holding in its curve
caricatures of goodness and right speech
and is it also true
that though wisdom
may sit among the sevenfold silences
she is hidden in smoke
so when she rises to approach us
it is hard to find her hands?

What Is Found

Waiting
you learn to hear her silent voicings

Going
you learn to sing what she intones

Knowing
you sense her leaves ecstatic stirrings

Saying
time of autumn, time of stones

Guessing
I try to know the smallest shiftings

Worlds
most likely fallen, though they glow

Trying
the time of waiting can be trying

Glimpses
Worlds arising can be known

Tell me
lord of light and also thunder

Regents
stars and whirlings through all nights

Crowning
nature's plenitude of ashes

Chaste penumbra
shading light

Moon
you rose on through the silver ashes

Merging
fully splendrous with the sea

Thrashing
waves unbraided roaring landward

Hollows
deep resounding (inmost lee)

Terebinthos

Found Terebinth, where the road
    goes curving, an Olive way
        near the place of marvels

                Chairs in the shade
                hold no wisdom
                    remember, drink water
                  heat can be sly

Terebinthos alone, memoria
    in marble; words drenched, dried,
        rushed into stone
            scratched, set-in, by-gone fanatics
                side by side, songs of the slaughtered

A clipped branch stands
  in a glass of water
    Thyme fills my room
      in unseen ways

                    The lives of nations
                        Breaking like ashes
                    The lives of men
                        Groping alone

And Terebinth Tree
  Near a field of broom
    Alone as by preference
      (the glorious noon)

We shade our feet
　While our hands keep on reaching
　　We hold our heads
　　　Lest GLARE
　　　　Come too soon

　　　　And O sacred Word
　　　　　Near the nations drifting
　　　　A man shoots a pistol
　　　　　Into the sea
　　　　　　Yet voices can speak
　　　　　　　Through shrines of a language
　　　　　　So as not to be sullied
　　　　　　　In unseen rooms

And Terebinth you, by balancing waters,
Acacia grows where the wind blows dry
And Olive trees spiralling in towards a manger
Sing Mimosa and Olive, Ash, Terebinth

You of the wind not risen

you breath in me

                hardly breathing

you live in me

                scarcely moving

If I give you a box of the sea-made stones

Will you draw your face in the summer sands

And winds from the east may you never come

Afterword

The Terebinth Tree is sometimes called the Mamre Oak. It is the tree under which Jacob dreamed. David slew Goliath in the Valley of the Terebinths. And to the Greeks, Persians, holding the Tree sacred, were known as Terebinths.

This is a book of poems and stone fragments.

I have interspersed the fragments among poems and poetic sequences, with the understanding that what occurs between the poems, or among them, is a least as important as what the poems themselves contain.

Thus there are three elements – poems, fragments and the spaces between.

g.w.